Cooking with F.R.

Recipes for Food That Appeared on That Epic Show

BY: Maya Colt

MAYA COLT

Copyright Page

Table of Contents

Prologue

When it comes to TV shows, F.R.I.E.N.D.S. has ruled the roost for possibly longer than any other sitcom. No matter what the situation, there's probably a FRIENDS' quote that will perfectly fit! Whether it's the goofy "How you doing?" from Joey or singing Phoebe's "Smelly Cat" in the shower, I've always been a huge fan of the show.

The bonds of friendship that the characters share with each other have become subjects of dinner table discussions, memes, and what not! While each character in that show was memorable, I have to be honest here… Monica has always been the character closed to my heart, possibly because she and I are both chefs. We also tend to mother our group and make sure that there's always food in the fridge and everyone is well fed…

While coffee was the biggest part of the show, and almost a character in itself, Monica made sure that we also pay attention to the food. This cookbook is almost a dedication to Mon, and to thank her for all the times she inspired me to whip up a storm!

The recipes in this book are super easy and simplified so that anyone who has the most basic equipment can cook! And while I can't promise that they will be as "to-die-for" as Monica Geller, I can definitely assure you that they will bring back amazing memories of watching this iconic show.

Drinks

The Tiki Death Punch

Remember in the first season when Monica asked Rachel if she wanted some Tiki Death Punch? Well, the only thing we know about the drink is that it has Rum and it's a Pink-Red shade... I know that isn't much to go on with, but I figured I'd give you my interpretation of this drink that has become the stuff of legends!

Serves 4

Time: 10 minutes

Ingredients

- 60 ml Dark Coconut Rum
- 60 ml Gold Rum
- 60 ml Pineapple/Mango flavoured Rum
- 120 ml Strawberry Syrup or Watermelon Syrup
- 250 ml Pineapple Juice
- Juice of 1 large lime

To Garnish: Fresh fruit such as a slice of pineapple or lime and some mint

Method

1. Throw all the ingredients in a blender and blend together till everything is uniformly mixed.

2. Pour in a tall glass over some ice.

3. Garnish with lime or pineapple and mint.

4. Serve immediately!

Phoebe's Vacation Mimosas

There's no one quite like Phoebe. She's a girl after my own heart. And when she drank mimosas for breakfast in Season 6 after the ill-fated Vegas wedding of Ross and Rachel, I thought to myself, "Girl, Smelly cat or not, I love you!" Mimosas are easy to make and delicious, especially if you're lounging by the pool, on a well-deserved holiday! Make them by the pitcher and enjoy!

Serves 4

Time: 10 minutes

Mimosas are usually a 2 ingredient cocktail- orange juice and sparkling wine. I suggest prosecco because it goes beautifully with the citrus taste, and it is cheap. I don't like to use expensive champagne for this recipe because we'll be diluting it with juice anyway.

Depending on my mood, I love to vary the juice I'm using. You can try grapefruit, cranberry, or even watermelon juice instead of the traditional orange. Throw in a sprig of thyme or sage if you're feeling adventurous.

Ingredients

- 700 ml Prosecco
- 350 ml Orange Juice, without pulp
- Ice
- Lime Wedges, to garnish

Method

1. Ensure that your ingredients are chilled.

2. Hold your glass at a slant and pour the bubbly in slowly, till about 2/3rd of the glass is full.

3. Top up with Orange juice till full.

4. Do not stir the drink, otherwise the bubbles will evaporate too soon.

5. Garnish with lime wedges and herbs.

Margaritas

I remember watching Ross drown his sorrows in Fajitas and Margaritas, and thinking to myself 'Fajitas and Margaritas' would be a great party theme! LOL, I'm yet to throw that party, but I've lost count of the number of times I've used this recipe! PS: There's a recipe for Fajitas in this book too.

Makes 1 pitcher

Time: 10 minutes

Ingredients

- 3 cups mid-range Tequila (Don't use the cheap stuff for this one!)
- 1 cup Triple Sec
- 1 cup Orange Juice
- 1 cup Lime or Lemon Juice (Freshly-squeezed is best!)
- ½ cup Simple Syrup

To Garnish: a slice of lime for each glass

Method

1. Combine all the ingredients except the Simple Syrup.

2. Add Simple Syrup according to taste. I prefer a slightly sweet taste, so I used about half a cup. But you do you, boo…

3. If you want a salt rim around each glass, run a wedge of lime/lemon around the edge and dip into a container with salt. Make sure to chill your glasses before you serve.

4. Pour over ice and serve.

Coffee

Probably should have started with this one! Coffee at Central Perk was almost a character in itself, for the amount of times and ways it contributed to the show. Americans do drink their coffee differently from other countries, but here's a special section dedicated to every lover of the show, ever!

Makes 2 cups

Time: 10 minutes

Ingredients

- 4 tbsp medium grind coffee
- 12 ounces water (cold filtered is best)

Method

1. Boil the water. Once the water has boiled, let it sit for 30-40 seconds.

Boiling water is way too hot to get the best flavor from your coffee.

2. If you're using a coffee filter or a French Press, add the coffee, and gently pour a little water onto the grind, enough to wet them but not drown them.

3. Let the coffee bloom for about a minute, and then pour the remaining water on the coffee.

4. If you are using a French Press, let the coffee steep for a couple of minutes before drinking.

Everything Else

Thanksgiving Sandwich aka The Moist Maker

One of my favorite episodes ever was the ninth episode of the fifth season. You may remember it as the one with the sandwich, more specifically Ross' Thanksgiving leftovers sandwich. This is my attempt at recreating a Monica Geller masterpiece!

Serves 1

Time: 10 minutes

Ingredients

- 3 slices, Bread
- 2-3 slices, leftover Turkey Meat
- ½ cup, leftover Gravy
- 2 tbsp leftover mashed potato OR
- 2 tbsp leftover stuffing
- 1 tbsp cranberry sauce
- A few leaves of lettuce
- 2 slices of fresh tomato
- Butter

Method

1. Butter two slices of bread. Soak one slice in gravy.

2. Layer the lettuce, tomato, and stuffing/mashed potato, on the bottom layer.

3. Put the gravy soaked slice on top of the bottom layer.

4. Lay the turkey slices on top of the gravy soaked layer.

5. Gently spread the cranberry sauce on top and cover with the last slice of buttered bread.

Phoebe's Grandma's Cookies

This episode was another one of my favourites. I mean, every girl has probably tried to distract herself from a painful breakup by doing something she loves and totally going overboard in the process. Anyway, back to Phoebe's French Great Grandmother, Nestle Toulouse, and her amazing cookies. Well, this may not be the exact recipe from the back of a packet, but it is pretty darn good!

Makes 12 cookies approximately

Time: 20 minutes

Ingredients

- 2/3 cup plain flour
- ¼ cup white sugar
- ¼ cup brown sugar
- ¼ cup soft butter
- 1 small egg or ½ large egg
- ¼ tsp baking soda
- ½ tsp vanilla extract
- ½ cup Nestle Toll House Chocolate Morsels
- ¼ tsp salt (omit if using salted butter)

Method

1. Preheat oven to 350 degree F.

2. Mix the following dry ingredients in a bowl- flour, baking soda, and salt.

3. In another bowl, (or in the bowl of a stand mixer, if you have one), beat the softened butter and sugar till light and airy.

4. Add the egg and vanilla extract and continue to beat till the egg is completely combined.

5. Add the flour in 2 batches and beat on a low speed to mix well.

6. Add the chocolate bits and stir with a spatula to evenly distribute.

7. Rest the dough for at least 20 minutes, to prevent the cookies from spreading too much in the oven.

8. Take out from the fridge and place even sized balls on a baking tray. Remember to grease the tray or line with baking paper beforehand.

9. Bake for about 10 minutes. They should be an even brown colour, not too dark and not too light. Cool completely on a wire rack before eating.

Quiche

While this recipe does not involve any blue fingernails, it is pretty gorgeous looking and so versatile. Use whatever leftovers you have in the fridge as filling. I've used smoked chicken, roast veggies, roast ham and what not, to great success. As long as you get the egg to cream ratio right, there's very little that you can mess up here. So, no need to worry that you may 'pull a Monica'! LOL!

Makes 1x 20 cm Quiche

Time: 1.5 hours

Ingredients

- 1 sheet savoury short pastry
- 3 eggs
- ½ cup milk
- ½ cup cream
- 1 cup filling of your choice
- ½ cup grated cheese (I love a cheddar-
- mozzarella blend or something smoky!
- Salt & Pepper to taste

Method

1. Preheat oven to 375 degree F.

2. Grease your dish, and line with the pastry.

3. Whisk the remaining ingredients together and set aside.

4. Bake the pastry for about 15 minutes, or until golden brown.

5. Take out of the oven, carefully pour the egg mix in, and return to the oven.

6. Lower the temperature to about 300 degree F, and bake for 30-35 minutes, depending on your oven. Allow to cool completely before slicing.

The quiche is done when the sides are firm but the middle is slightly wobbly. The middle will continue to cook as the quiche cools down. The top should be an even golden brown and the pastry should be slightly crunchy.

Thanksgiving Mac n Cheese

It's no secret that Chandler hated all things Thanksgiving, and who can blame the poor guy. Anyway, I found it so cute that Monica made him something so American in lieu of turkey and the works. I'm pretty sure she became a chef partly because of Chandler's off-hand comment after he tasted her mac and cheese. This recipe is dedicated to that episode!

Serves 2 hungry people

Time: 1 hour

Ingredients

- ½ cup macaroni
- 1 tbsp olive oil
- 2 tbsp butter
- 1 tbsp plain flour
- ½ cup milk
- ½ cup cream
- 1 cup grated cheese (use your favourite melting cheese. I love an aged cheddar)
- ½ tsp garlic powder
- ½ tsp smoked paprika
- Salt & Pepper to taste

Optional:

- ¼ cup breadcrumbs or Panko crumb, if you have any
- 1 tbsp melted butter
- ¼ cup grated cheese

Method

1. Preheat the oven to 350 degree F.

2. Boil water in a pot and cook pasta till al dente.

3. Refresh with cold water, and strain carefully. Add oil to the pasta and let it cool.

4. In a pan over medium heat, add the butter and flour, and cook till the flour is golden brown.

5. Whisk in the milk and cream and continue to stir until fully combined.

6. Lower the heat and add the cheese, paprika, and garlic powder. Season to taste.

7. Whisk until the cheese has melted.

8. Add the cooked pasta and stir until the macaroni is completed coated in the sauce.

9. If using the optional ingredients, carefully tip the macaroni into an oven safe dish.

10. In a separate bowl, combine the breadcrumbs, melted butter and cheese. Top the macaroni with this mix.

11. Bake for about 20 minutes or till the breadcrumbs are golden brown and the cheese has melted completely.

Birthday Flan

To be fair, most people wouldn't do a flan instead of cake on a birthday. But then, this is Monica we're talking about. She's got a sense of flair, that woman! You won't hear me complaining if someone got me a birthday flan. This recipe is easy to make and so delicious that you won't go back to the plain cake after this!

Makes 1x 8 inch flan

Time: 3.5 hours

Ingredients

- 6 eggs
- ½ cup brown sugar
- 2 tsp Vanilla extract
- 30 oz (900 ml) Milk
- 1 cup white sugar
- ¼ cup water

Method

1. Preheat the oven to 265 degree F. Prepare a water bath by filling a deep tray capable of holding the tin you're using for the flan.

2. In a saucepan, combine the white sugar and water, and stir gently to lightly dissolve.

3. Place the saucepan on a low heat and do not stir anymore, or else your caramel will crystalize into chunks. If you see sugar sticking to the sides of the pan, use a pastry brush dipped in water to lightly brush the sides.

4. Allow the caramel to turn a golden amber color, nothing too dark.

5. In the meantime, gently heat the milk over a medium flame. Do not boil.

6. Gently whisk the eggs, brown sugar and vanilla extract in a separate bowl. Try not to make the egg mix too frothy.

7. The milk should be warm enough now. Gently pour into the egg mix and whisk with a light hand to combine. Strain into a jug to remove any egg bits.

8. When the caramel turns a deep golden, take it off the heat and carefully pour into the greased cake/pie tin you're using. Be careful, sugar burns are nasty!

9. Let it cool for a minute before you pour in the custard. The caramel will go slightly thick.

10. Pour the egg custard over the back of a spoon over the caramel. Pouring it over a spoon and not directly in helps the caramel to remain undisturbed.

11. Place the tin gently into the water bath. Cover the entire thing with tin foil.

12. Place in the oven and bake for about 30-35 minutes, depending on the oven. The custard should be slightly jiggly, as it will continue to cook while cooling.

13. When slightly set, remove from the oven but leave the tin in the water bath for another hour or until cool.

14. Place the tin in the fridge for another 1.5 hours.

15. When unmoulding, use a plate with a rim to catch the liquid caramel. Slide a warm knife along the edges of the tin. Plate the rimmed plate on top of the tin and flip it over to unmould the flan.

16. Don't worry if the edges slightly break, that is normal, and you'll get better with practise.

17. Decorate with whipped cream and fruit if you so desire.

Marshmallows

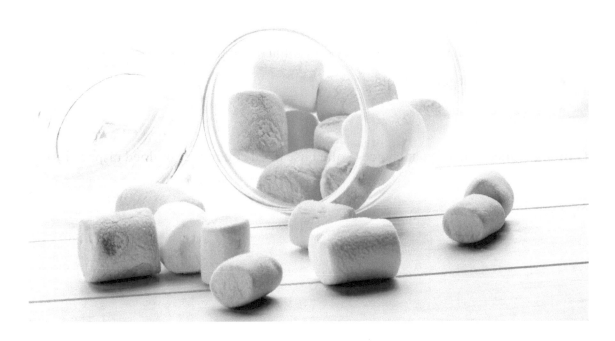

Remember when Rachel stuffed a marshmallow up Monica's nose? Ouch! Bet she wasn't holding these marshmallows, otherwise, she would have been eating them and not wasting them up to someone's nose! This recipe is very kid-friendly and is a crowd-pleaser.

Serves 8

Time: 20 mins

Ingredients

- 1 cup sugar
- ½ cup water
- 1 ½ tsp gelatine
- 4-5 drops of flavouring (I usually do vanilla or peppermint)
- 3-4 drops red gel food colour
- ½ cup icing sugar

Optional: Dried fruit of your choice (I often use dried cranberries or dried raspberries)

Method

1. Combine the sugar and water in a saucepan and heat till the sugar begins to dissolve.

2. While your sugar dissolves, add the gelatine to a bowl and add 1 ½ tbsp hot water. Stir and set aside to bloom.

3. Once the sugar has dissolved and the gelatine has softened, add the gelatine to the saucepan and stir to combine. There should be no lumps.

4. Bring this sugar syrup to the boil. If you have a candy thermometer, it should reach 240 F before you take it off the heat. If you don't have one, wait for the sugar syrup to boil rapidly with the bubbles becoming bigger and taking longer to pop. When you see this happening, take the saucepan off the heat and let it cool slightly.

5. Add to the bowl of a stand mixer or use a hand held mixer. Add the vanilla and food colour and start beating the sugar syrup at a low speed.

6. Continue to whisk, slowly increasing the speed as it becomes white and fluffy and doubles in size.

7. Lightly grease a pan and liberally dust with the icing sugar. Pour the marshmallow mix into the pan and allow to set for 15-20 mins.

OPTIONAL: If using dried fruit, pour half the mix into the pan. Sprinkle dried fruit on top, and then top with the remaining marshmallow mix.

8. Remove from pan and cut into desired shapes.

Thanksgiving Turkey

You can't have Thanksgiving without a Turkey, even if that turkey has been on your head for several hours! Joey called that his worst Thanksgiving... No horrible Thanksgivings with this recipe though! I can promise this one will make for great memories!

Serves 4

Time: 3.5 hours

Ingredients

- 1 fresh turkey, 10-12 pounds, cleaned with giblets removed, room temperature
- 1 stick butter
- 1 lemon, halved
- 4-5 cloves of garlic, crushed
- 1 small bunch parsley, chopped
- 2 sprigs rosemary, chopped
- 1 small bunch parsley, chopped
- Flaky Salt & pepper, to taste
- Oil to drizzle over

For the Stuffing

- 2 small onions, halved
- 1 head of garlic, halved through the middle
- 2-3 small sprigs rosemary

Method

1. Preheat your oven to 450 degree F.

2. Prepare the garlic butter by combining the butter, garlic and herbs in a bowl. Squeeze the juice of the lemon into the butter mix. Don't discard the lemon.

3. Whisk ingredients together to form a garlic herb butter.

4. Pat the turkey dry with some paper towels. Place into a heavy bottomed roasting pan that is deep enough to hold the turkey drippings.

5. Thoroughly season the inside of the turkey.

6. Gently separate the skin of the bird from the breast area by pushing your fingers underneath.

7. Rub the butter under the skin and on top, taking care to cover every bit of the turkey.

8. Stuff the cavity with the onions, squeezed lemon, head of garlic and rosemary. Tie the legs together with kitchen string.

9. Drizzle the oil generously over the turkey and sprinkle a little more salt on top to help crisp up the skin.

10. Bake for 20 mins at 430 F.

11. Baste the turkey with the melted butter in the tray every 20 minutes or so.

12. Lower the temperature to 350 degree F and bake for another 2 ½ hours. Continue to baste so keep the turkey from drying out.

13. Once cooked, remove from the oven and rest for at least 15-20 minutes before serving.

If you begin to carve the turkey immediately after removing from the oven, the juices will all run out and the turkey will become dry.

Cranberry Sauce, aka Chanberry Sauce

What would Thanksgiving be without fresh cranberry sauce? Of course, if you have Chandler helping, there's no way that the cranberry sauce isn't going to be subject to his quips. Ta-da, presenting the Chanberry Sauce! Easy and the perfect side to Thanksgiving Turkey!

Serves 4

Time: 30 mins

Ingredients

- 2 cups fresh cranberries, washed
- ½ cup water
- ½ cup sweetened Apple or Orange juice
- 1 cup brown sugar

Optional: ½ tsp orange zest

Method

1. Combine all the ingredients, except the cranberries in a heavy bottomed saucepan, on medium heat.

2. Stir to dissolve sugar.

3. Gently tip in the washed and picked through cranberries.

4. Lower the heat and cook for about 20 minutes or until the cranberries burst open. This sauce will be thick and chunky. If you like yours more runny, add a bit more water or juice.

5. Once soft and mushy, take off the heat and allow it to cool slightly. Add the optional orange zest when the sauce is still warm and let it rest, so that the orange notes can develop.

The Attack of the Hummus

Has anyone finally discovered "What gets out Hummus"? I loved Phoebe and her little hummus spat with Joey. With this recipe here, I can assure you that no one will be getting into hummus fights, coz no one will want to waste even a little bit of this beauty! I know you'll agree once you get a taste…

Serves 4

Time: 30 mins

Ingredients

- 1 can (15 ounce) chickpeas
- 4 tbsp tahini paste
- 4 large cloves of garlic
- ½ cup olive oil
- ¼ tsp cumin powder
- Juice of 1 lemon
- A couple of pinches Paprika
- Salt, to taste
- Chopped Parsley, to Garnish

Method

1. This will sound unusual but boil the canned chickpeas for about 10 minutes before blitzing them. This makes them a little creamier and easy to grind.

2. While the chickpeas are boiling, roast the garlic cloves in a pan over medium heat. Do not brown them too much, a light brown is perfect.

3. Strain the chickpeas and add to a food processor with all the other ingredients except the olive oil.

4. Puree in a food processor and pour the oil in slowly from the top, almost like you would make an emulsion for a salad dressing. This is a trick I learnt from a Turkish chef I worked for, and it does make for a creamy hummus.

5. Scrape the sides and season to taste. If the hummus is too thick, add a few more tablespoons of oil and continue to puree. The entire process should at least take 10 minutes, for that really creamy and soft hummus.

Garnish with paprika and chopped parsley.

Optional: I've used this basic recipe and tweaked it to make all kinds of flavoured hummus, including Roast Pumpkin Hummus, Bell Pepper Hummus, Avocado Hummus (this is one of my favourites!) and even Beetroot Hummus. To be honest, the only thing stopping you is your imagination! Set it free and see where it takes you!

Monica's Jam

Is there a better way to get over a man than to start your own jam business? Don't go answering that question before you get a taste of this recipe. I guarantee that you'll be spreading it on everything, just like Mr. Tribbiani! This one uses apples, which is the easiest fruit to work with if you're new to jam-making.

Serves 6 cups

Time: 1 hour

Ingredients

- 4 lbs fresh apples
- 2 cups sugar
- 4 tbsp fresh lemon juice
- 2 cinnamon sticks
- 3-4 whole star anise

Method

Apple jam is probably one of the easiest fruits to make into a jam because apples are naturally high in Pectin. Pectin is what helps jam set.

Method

1. Peel and core the apples.

2. Chop or slice them into small, equal sized portions.

3. Place in a heavy bottomed saucepan, on medium heat, and add enough water to cover the fruit.

4. Cook till the apples start getting slightly mushy.

5. Lower the heat. Add the sugar and continue to cook till the mixture has reduced and is thick. This should take about 25-30 minutes, depending on the heat of your stove.

6. Add the lemon juice, star anise, and cinnamon. Continue to cook for about 10 minutes more, on low heat.

7. The jam is ready if you drop a little bit on a cold surface and it holds its shape.

8. Remove the cinnamon and star anise. Cool completely before transferring to bottles.

Rachel's Trifle (Without the Meat!)

Poor Rachel, at least she tried! I mean, Joey liked it, didn't he? After all, "I mean, what's not to like? Custard, good. Jam, good. Meat, good!". Well, this recipe is a little more vegetarian, it certainly doesn't have minced beef in it, but I'd say it's still pretty good! Here's my Black Forest Trifle, perfect for a dinner party.

Serves 10

Time: 2 hours

Ingredients

- 1 chocolate sponge (Feel free to use a store bought one here)
- ½ cup kirsch or cherry brandy
- 6 cups of sweetened whipped cream
- 3 cups fresh cherries, roughly sliced
- Chocolate shavings, to garnish
- 5-8 whole fresh cherries, to garnish

Method

1. Slice through the chocolate sponge cake to divide into two thinner layers.

2. Brush both layers liberally with the kirsch or brandy. I use half a cup but if you want yours slightly more boozy, feel free to adjust this to your taste.

2. Take the dish you are using for your trifle and add 1 cup of whipped cream to the bottom. Sprinkle 1 cup of cherry slices on the whipped cream.

3. Place one of the chocolate sponge layers on top.

4. Pour 3 cups of the whipped cream on top. Top with 2 cups of sliced cherries.

5. Gently place the other sponge layer on top and repeat the layering steps with the remaining 2 cups of cream.

7. Top with the whole cherries and chocolate reserved for garnish.

8. Allow to chill for at least an hour before serving.

Joey's Meatball Subs

You can't watch the show and not observe that Joey eats a LOT of Meatball Subs! He's absolutely addicted to the things! I don't blame him. Meatball Subs can be delicious if made with the right **Ingredients**. This recipe below is my favourite and it is so easy to make!

Serves 1

Time: 1 hour

Ingredients

For the Meatballs

- 1 lb beef mince, room temperature
- 1 tbsp onion powder
- 1 tsp garlic powder
- 2 tsp mixed dried herbs
- 2 tbsp BBQ sauce
- 1 tbsp tomato ketchup
- 1 egg
- ½ cup breadcrumbs
- 1 medium sized onion, finely chopped
- Salt and Pepper, to season

Other Ingredients

- 3 tbsp oil
- 1 bread roll
- 1 ½ cups pizza sauce
- ½ cup shredded cheese (I use mozzarella)

Optional: A few leaves of Fresh Basil

Method

This will make quite a few meatballs, but we will only use 3 per sub. These freeze well, just in case you can't eat them all in one sitting!

1. Preheat the oven to 350 degrees F.

2. To make the meatballs, add all the ingredients to a big bowl and mix till properly combined. Do not overwork the meat.

3. Rest for about 15 minutes and then roll into small balls.

4. Add the oil to a pan over a medium heat. Gently place meatballs in the pan and fry for about 1-1.5 minutes on each side, depending on the size of the meatballs.

5. Once golden brown, lower the heat and add the pizza sauce to the pan. Simmer for another 7-10 minutes or until the meatballs are soft and cooked throughout. Remove from heat.

6. Slit the bread roll but not all the way through.

7. Add 3-4 meatballs per bread roll as per your liking.

8. Add the cheese on top carefully and place on an oven tray.

9. Take out as soon as cheese has melted, usually in a couple of minutes, depending on your oven.

10. Sprinkle the fresh basil leaves, if you've got any and serve hot!

Monica's Christmas Candies

Who wouldn't want Monica as a neighbour? The homemade Christmas candies themselves would be a good enough reason. And who knows, if you were nice to her, maybe she'd even invite you over for dinner sometime! Wowzah! While I wait for a Monica to show up in my life, how about you try my recipe for homemade candy?

Serves 15

Time: 1 hour

Ingredients

- 2 cups plain milk or dark chocolate, melted
- 2 cups mixed nuts, fruit, marshmallows (really, you can use any filling you want to, as long as it isn't too watery)

Optional: 1 cup white chocolate

Method

1. Grease a chocolate mold, and carefully pour a teaspoon of melted chocolate into each mould.

Alternatively, if you have any piping bags at home, fill the melted chocolate into the pipping bag and pipe melted chocolate into each mold carefully.

2. After you've filled all the molds in the tray, flip the mold over a tray to get rid of the excess chocolate inside each mold.

3. Place the mold inside the freezer for about 10-15 minutes and allow the chocolate to harden slightly.

4. After the chocolate has hardened, remove from freezer. Carefully add a little filling to each mold.

5. Top the filling with more melted chocolate and smoothen out so that the mold is completely even and covered.

6. Return to the freezer for another 20-30 mins.

7. When the chocolate has hardened, remove from the molds by carefully flipping the mould.

8. OPTIONAL: Pipe or drizzle melted white chocolate over each piece to decorate.

9. Store in the refrigerator.

Mrs. Braverman's Cheesecake

Imagine eating cheesecake off the floor because it's too good to resist! LOL, hopefully, after you've made my version of a baked cheesecake, you'll cut the cake a slice, place it on a plate and still agree that it's the best cheesecake you've ever made! I've left this one plain, but feel free to add fruit or other dessert toppings!

Serves 12

Time: 6 hours (including chilling time)

Ingredients

For the Base

- 8 oz biscuit crumbs (feel free to use chocolate or vanilla, depending on your preference)
- 10 tbsp melted butter

For the Filling

- 1 lb Cream Cheese, room temperature
- 2 tbsp Plain Flour
- ½ cup Sour Cream
- 2 tbsp Vanilla extract
- 1 ½ cups white sugar
- 2 tbsp lemon juice (freshly squeezed, if possible)
- 4 tbsp finely grated lemon zest
- 3 eggs, room temperature

Method

1. Preheat oven to 295 degree F (fan-forced) or 320 degree F (standard).

2. Line an 8 inch springform tin with baking paper. Clip the bottom over a large piece of paper, so that the excess paper sides stick out. This helps in sliding off the baked cheesecake later.

3. Mix the biscuit crumb and butter and press this mix firmly into the tin. Use the back of a large spatula to flatten, if necessary.

4. Allow to chill in the fridge, while you start on the filling.

5. Into the bowl of your stand mixer, add the cream cheese, flour, sour cream, sugar, vanilla, lemon juice, lemon zest and flour. Beat until just combined. DO NOT OVER BEAT since this will create aeration and cause the cheesecake to rise and then crack while baking. Stop beating when you can't make out individual ingredients.

6. Gently beat in the eggs, one at a time. Again, beat until just combined.

7. Take the prepared springform tin out of the fridge. By now the base should have hardened.

8. Carefully pour the cheesecake filling into the tin.

9. Place into oven and bake for 50 minutes. The centre should jiggle slightly. It will continue to firm up later.

PRO TIP: Add a pan of water to the oven when baking: place a tray of water in the oven on the lowest shelf and place the cheesecake on a middle shelf. This will help prevent cracking.

10. Turn the oven off and leave the cheesecake in the oven, with the door slightly open for another 2 hours till the cheesecake is cooler and more stable.

11. Place in the fridge for another couple of hours until completely chilled.

12. TO UNMOULD: Place the tin on something with a little height on your table/kitchen counter. That way, when you unclip the tin, you don't need to worry about the sides catching.

Take the plate off and use the excess paper sides to slide onto a serving plate.

13. Decorate with optional fruit or dessert toppings or eat as is.

Bologna Sandwich

Joey loves his sandwiches, there's no doubting that! This Bologna Sandwich is an ode to Joey, the perfect goofy addition to any gang of friends! This recipe is super quick and **Makes** for a great snack or lunch!

Serves 1

Time: 20 minutes

Ingredients

- 4 slices Bologna
- 2 slices bread
- 2 slices cheese
- 1 pickle, thinly sliced
- 1 tbsp mayonnaise
- 1 tbsp spicy mustard
- 1 tsp oil

Method

1. Heat the oil in a pan on medium heat.

2. Fry the slices of bologna on each side till crispy on the edges.

3. Remove the pan from the heat and reserve the fat in the pan.

4. Spread the mayo on one slice of bread and the mustard on the other.

5. Layer the Bologna, Cheese and pickles in between the two slices of bread.

6. Heat the pan with the fat. Place the sandwich gently into the pan and cook till golden brown on both sides.

7. Serve hot!

Joey's Ice-Cream from His Fridge

Remember that time when Joey's fridge went off and he decided to eat everything in it, including the centuries-old ice cream? Well, I don't know if you want that funky taste in your mouth, but I promise that you'll love this Orange and Kahlua ice cream recipe of mine!

Serves 4

Time: 6 hours

Ingredients

- 20 oz cream
- 1 (13.4 oz) tin Dulce de Leche (Caramel)
- 6 tbsp Kahlua
- 4 tbsp instant coffee
- Zest of 2 oranges

Method

1. Whisk caramel till smooth in a large bowl.

2. Dissolve the coffee granules in Kahlua. Whisk into the caramel.

3. Add cream to the caramel mix. Whisk till airy and soft peak stage is reached. Use an electronic hand mixer or a stand mixer to do this.

4. Transfer to air tight container and freeze for at least 6 hours or preferably overnight.

5. Scoop and serve as a side or on its own.

Joey's Pizza

Joey is honestly a man after my own heart. How can you not love a guy who loves to eat? LOL, maybe he doesn't share his food, but Joey is every chef's nightmare and dream rolled into one! Here's my take on an Italian classic. Hopefully, Mr. Tribbiani Jr. likes it.

Makes 3 pizza

Time: 1.5 hours

Ingredients

For the Dough

- 1½ cups, warm water
- 4 cups, plain flour
- ½ cup, flour for dusting
- 1 sachet dried yeast
- A couple of pinches of sugar
- ½ tsp salt
- ½ cup oil (I prefer olive)

For the Pizza

- 2 cups pizza sauce or crème fraiche
- 3 cups mozzarella cheese
- 2 cups toppings of your choice

Method

1. Preheat the oven to 475 degree F. Prepare your starter by combining the water, yeast, sugar and a couple pinches of flour in a clean metal bowl. Cover the bowl with clingwrap and place in a warm place. A metal bowl is recommended because of its ability to absorb heat.

The yeast mix is ready to use when frothy and the clingwrap has become a small dome over the bowl.

2. Mix the flour and salt in a large bowl. Pour the yeast starter and half the oil in and use your hands to work it into a dough.

3. Dip your fingers into the remaining oil and generously dab it all over the dough. Turn the dough onto a flat surface and work for about 10 minutes until the dough is smooth and glossy.

4. Grease a bowl and put the dough into this bowl. Brush the surface of the dough lightly with some oil.

5. Cover with clingwrap and place in a warm place, so that the dough can rise and double in size.

6. Remove dough from bowl and work it into a long roll. Cut into sections and roll each section into a 20cm circle. The dough should easily make 3 pizzas.

7. Place the pizza base on a baking tray.

8. Leaving a half inch around the edges, spread a little pizza sauce or crème fraiche on the base. The mentioned 2 cups are for 3 pizzas.

9. Sprinkle cheese generously on top of the sauce.

10. Add desired toppings and sprinkle some more cheese on top.

11. Bake for about 10-15 minutes, depending on your oven. The pizza is done when the sides turn a crisp golden.

12. Garnish with fresh basil if you have any and serve hot!

All Things Fried with Cheese: Stuffed Mozzarella Sticks

I've always wondered where all the food Joey ate went. I mean, it certainly wasn't on his tummy or hips, which is where fat appears even if I so much as look at fried-food. But anyway, this recipe is my favourite version of fried-food with cheese in it! And you can even use the meatball mix from the Meatball Sub recipe!

Serves 6

Time: 30 minutes

Ingredients

For the Stuffing

- 1 lb beef or pork mince
- 1 medium sized onion, finely chopped
- 1 tbsp garlic powder
- 1 egg
- 1 tbsp mixed herbs
- 2 tbsp parsley (fresh or dried)
- 6 cheese sticks (string cheese is perfect)

For the Coating

- 1 cup, plain flour
- 2 eggs, beaten
- 1 cup breadcrumbs
- Oil, to fry

Method

1. Mix all the stuffing ingredients except the cheese, in a large bowl.

2. Take a good sized ball of the meat mix and flatten it out on your palm.

3. Put one cheese stick in the middle and fold over the meat mix to cover the cheese.

4. Mold into a long cylindrical shape.

5. In 3 separate bowls, lay out the flour, eggs and breadcrumbs.

6. Lay the meat stick in the floor, gently coat.

7. Dust off the extra flour and coat with egg. Then place the meat stick in the breadcrumbs and coat well.

8. Heat oil in a saucepan. Ensure the oil is hot before you gently drop in the meat stick into the oil. Cold oil will make the coating soak up more grease and make it super oily.

9. Cook till a medium golden brown on all sides. Drain oil.

10. Serve hot with tomato chutney!

Crab Cakes

Remember how in Season 9, episode 14, Ross and Joey try to score free crab cakes? That episode was hilarious and I loved that Joey and Phoebe were trying so hard to get Ross and Rachel back together! Anyway, these crab cakes are my mother's favourite and I wanted to share it with you too!

Serves 3

Time: 1.5 hours

Ingredients

- 2 cups cooked lump crab meat
- ¼ cup mashed potatoes
- ¼ cup cracker crumbs
- 2 tbsp fresh parsley, chopped
- 2 tsp fresh lemon juice
- 1 tsp lemon zest
- 2 tsp mustard
- 3 tbsp plain mayo
- ½ tsp smoked paprika
- 1 tsp fresh dill (OPTIONAL)
- 1 tsp finely chopped capers (OPTIONAL)
- Salt and pepper, to taste

Method

1. Preheat the oven to 450 degree F.

2. Place all the ingredients in a bowl, except for the crab meat and the cracker crumbs.

3. Mix well. Gently add the crab meat and crumb and mix with a folding motion. Don't stir vigorously otherwise all the crab meat will break and you'll end up with crab mush.

4. Refrigerate for at least 45 minutes to let the mix firm up. This makes it easier to shape.

5. Remove from the refrigerator and gently shape into large equal sized balls. Make sure no extra bits are sticking out. Flatten slightly.

6. Place onto greased tray and brush with butter if you'd like the crab cakes slightly crispy. Bake for 13-15 minutes, depending on your oven. The crab cakes are done when they are golden brown.

7. Serve with aioli or tartar sauce.

The Perv Salad

I can't remember if Monica took the creepy guy's job after making him that Perv Salad in Season 2, episode 14. I'm going to rewatch that episode, but in the meantime, why don't you try your hand at this salad too? It is simple, delicious, and super fresh! Oh, and it's not dirty at all!

Serves 1

Time: 20 mins

Ingredients

- 1 handful fresh lettuce leaves
- 5 cherry tomatoes, halved
- 3-4 cubes watermelon
- 6-8 blueberries
- ½ cup shredded chicken or prawns or tofu
- ¼ cup feta
- Olive oil, to drizzle OR Salad dressing

Method

1. Lay the lettuce down in a salad bowl.

2. In a separate bowl, mix the cherry tomatoes, watermelon, blueberries, chicken (or protein of your choice) and dressing or oil.

3. Add this mix to the lettuce leaves.

4. Crumble Feta on top.

5. Drizzle a little more olive oil on top and serve!

Tacos

I really don't believe that there can be anyone in this world who doesn't like tacos! Can't fault for Ross and Joey stopping on their way to Disneyland for a bite of deliciousness. Speaking of deliciousness, this recipe for pulled pork tacos is amazing and so, so easy to make! Take a look and tell me you don't agree! I've not included a recipe for pulled pork because this cookbook is a fun take on food and I don't want to complicate things. So, feel free to use bought pulled pork or through some pork shoulder into a slow cooker with some spices and BBQ sauce and you're all set!

Serves 2

Time: 20 mins

Ingredients

- 2 tortillas
- 1 ½ cups pulled pork
- ½ cup pineapple, small dices
- ½ cup red onion, small dices
- 2 tbsp lemon juice
- 1 cup shredded lettuce or cabbage
- ½ cup sour cream
- ¼ cup feta
- ½ small bunch of cilantro
- Lime Wedges

Optional: Jalapeno slices

Method

1. Make your salsa first, by combining the pineapple, onion, lemon juice, jalapenos and half the cilantro. Set aside.

2. Make the sauce to drizzle on top by blending the sour cream and feta together. If it is too thick, add a few tablespoons of milk or cream and blend to a pourable consistency.

3. Warm the tortillas. Add a layer of pulled pork to each.

4. Top with salsa and cabbage or lettuce. Drizzle feta sauce over the lettuce.

5. Sprinkle remaining cilantro on top.

6. Serve immediately with lime wedges on the side.

Key Lime Pie

Key Lime Pie is such a simple dessert to make, and you probably have all the ingredients lying in your pantry anyway. And if you've always wondered what the guys were eating when Chandler was making fun of Monica for making Ben cry (S2, E6), it was this gorgeous thing!

Serves 8

Time: 1 hour

Ingredients

- 2 cups biscuit crumb
- 1 cup melted butter
- 1 can (14 oz) sweetened condensed milk
- 4 limes, juiced
- Zest of 4 limes
- 2 cups cream
- 2 tbsp icing sugar
- Thinly sliced lime slices, to garnish

Method

1. Preheat oven to 320 degree F.

2. Mix the biscuit crumb and butter and press down firmly in a pie dish. Ensure the sides and bottom are uniformly thick.

3. Bake for about 15 minutes or until golden. Remove from the oven and cool.

4. In a bowl (use either an electric hand mixer or a stand mixer), add the egg yolks and whisk till creamy and pale.

5. Slowly drizzle in the condensed milk and continue to whisk for another 4-5 minutes.

6. Add the lime juice and zest and whisk for 3-4 minutes.

7. Pour the filling into the cool base and bake for about 15 minutes.

8. The centre will still be slightly jiggly but the outer parts will be set. Place in the fridge for at least 3-4 hours to cool.

9. Whip the cream with the icing sugar and spoon on top of the chilled pie. Garnish with lime slices and serve chilled.

Breakfast Muffins

Wouldn't it be nice if you and your friends could have breakfast together every other day, with a nice spread of muffins and coffee and toast, Anyway, here's a recipe for some not too sweet muffins to start your day.

Serves 6

Time: 40 minutes

Ingredients

- ¾ cup sugar
- 1 cup plain flour
- ¼ tsp salt
- 1 egg
- ½ cup oil
- 1 ½ cups milk
- 1 ½ cup blueberries or chocolate chips
- 2 tsp lemon or orange zest
- 2 tsp baking powder

Method

1. Preheat oven to 350 degree F.

2. In a mixing bowl, mix the flour, sugar, salt and baking powder.

3. In a separate bowl, whisk together the oil, egg and milk. Don't worry if the oil floats on top, it will.

4. Add the liquid to the flour mix and gently stir to combine. Don't over whisk, otherwise the muffins will become tough.

5. Add the berries or cholate and zest and gently fold into the muffin batter.

6. Pour into greased muffin tins and bake for about 18-20 minutes. A skewer inserted into the centre of the muffin should come out clean.

7. Dust with a little icing sugar if desired and serve!

Scones

Scones and coffee are a match made in heaven! This scone recipe is such a winner! It can be made with the simplest of Ingredients and is practically a no-fail recipe! Take a chance with this one and I can assure you, you won't ever need another recipe!

Serves 2

Time: 30 minutes

Ingredients

- 2 cups self-rising flour
- 1 cup cream
- 1 egg
- 1½ cups shredded cheese
- 2 tbsp herbs
- 3-4 tbsp milk

Method

1. Preheat the oven to 350 degree F.

2. In a mixing bowl, add the flour, cheese, and herbs and mix well.

3. Whish the cream and eggs together and pour into the flour mix and knead to a soft dough.

4. Don't over work the dough, or the scones will become tough and chewy.

5. Turn onto a floured surface. The dough will be slightly sticky, that's normal.

6. Pat into a circle and cut into wedges.

7. Place on a tray lined with baking paper.

8. Brush with milk and sprinkle a little cheese on top of each wedge.

9. Bake for approximately 15 minutes, until the scones have risen and are golden brown.

10. Serve warm with butter.

Fajitas

These are a Tex-Mex favourite and I can see why! Although Ross went kinda overboard with his Fajitas and Margaritas double date dinner, I love how he tried to act "normal" in front of the other three! Poor thing though, burning his hands like that… Anyway, these fajitas are chicken ones, but feel free to sub the protein for anything else you'd prefer!

Serves 4

Time: 35 minutes

Ingredients

- 4 tortillas
- 5 tbsp oil
- ½ cup sliced red bell peppers
- ½ cup sliced yellow bell peppers
- ½ cup sliced green bell peppers
- ½ cup sliced onions
- 3 chicken breasts, cut into strips
- ½ cup sour cream

For the Spice Blend

- 1 tbsp dried oregano
- 1 tsp ground cumin
- 1 tsp ground coriander
- 1 tsp garlic powder
- 1 tsp onion powder
- 1 tsp smoked paprika
- ½ tsp chilli flakes
- 2 tsp lemon juice
- Salt to taste

Optional:

- 1 cup Grated cheese
- 2 avocados or 1 cup guacamole

Ingredients

1. Marinate the chicken with all the spice blend ingredients. Rest for 20 minutes.

2. While the chicken is marinating, in a hot pan with half the oil, stir fry the bell peppers and onions. Remove when slightly tender.

3. In the same pan, add the remaining oil and cook the chicken thoroughly. Add the bell peppers mix in to the pan once the chicken is cooked.

4. Warm the tortillas (in a pan or microwave). Divide the chicken filling equally and spoon into the centre of each tortilla.

5. Add sour cream on top and other optional toppings if using.

6. Serve hot!

Monica's Lasagne in An Hour

I mean, save the best for the last, right? Monica's lasagne is legendary and appears in almost every season. Well, there's always some in her freezer too, if I remember correctly. Lasagne is a lot easier than it looks. This one is a breeze and can be made ahead and frozen for those days when you don't feel like cooking anything!

Serves 4

Time: 1 hour

Ingredients

- 1 lb beef mince
- 3 tbsp oil
- 1 large onion, finely chopped
- 2 large cloves garlic, minced
- 1½ cups vegetables (celery, carrot, mushrooms, leeks, anything you have at home)
- 2 tbsp fresh parsley, chopped
- 1 small handful basil leaves
- 2 cups pasta sauce
- ½ cup beef stock
- 1 cup cottage cheese
- 1 cup cream cheese
- 1 cup grated cheese (any melting variety is fine)
- 3 sheets fresh lasagne
- Salt to taste

Method

1. Preheat the oven to 350 degree F.

2. In a large pan, heat the oil and then sauté the onions and garlic.

3. Once softened, add the vegetables and mince. Cook till evenly brown.

4. Add the pasta sauce, herbs and stock. Mix well. Simmer for about 10-15 minutes till the sauce is thick.

5. While the sauce is simmering, blend the cottage cheese and cream cheese together. This is the cheese sauce we'll use.

6. Cut the lasagne sheets to the size of the dish you intend to use.

7. Once the mince is done, start layering the lasagne. Start with 1/3rd of the meat sauce at the bottom and spoon some of the cheese sauce over the mince. Sprinkle 1/3rd of the grated cheese. Top with a sheet of lasagne.

8. Repeat the layers with remaining ingredients. Remember to spread grated cheese on top for a beautiful bubbling golden top layer.

9. Cover the dish with foil and bake in the oven for 30 minutes.

10. Remove the foil after the 30 minutes and bake for another 5-10 minutes to ensure the cheese melts completely.

11. Serve hot with a small side salad!

Epilogue

Writing this book brought back a lot of good memories of binge-watching the show. I still can't believe that it has been more than 10 years since the pilot episode aired. I am very glad I got to revisit some of the best episodes through one of my greatest loves- food! In fact, I'm pretty sure that one of the reasons why I love Monica so much, is because she is a chef and a lover of all thing gourmet!

I hope you have a fabulous time making the recipes in this book and perhaps sharing these meals with your gang of amazing friends, while laughing and remembering all the good times you guys have been through together.

After all, isn't that what friendship and good food are meant to do anyway? Bring people together in the best and worst times in their lives. Till next time… I'll be there for you!

Author's Afterthoughts

Thank you very much for buying this book. I am so thankful for taking the time to read it. The reason why I write is not only because I love writing, the reason is you. I enjoy helping people and writing is the best way to do it. Plus you know how to cherish every word you read.

How did you choose this book? There are so many books and authors on same/similar topics and you still stopped at my book and decided to get it. I am so grateful! I know that you made an amazing decision and you will get great benefits from reading.

Now, tell me what you think about the book? Authors grow and become better thanks to the feedback of their readers. I will appreciate taking a minute to leave even small feedback. Everything counts! Plus, you might even be an inspiration to other readers.

Thank you again

Maya Colt

About the Author

Maya Colt didn't have an easy journey. She knew that she loved cooking but she didn't have a chance to focus on college right after high school. Instead, she started working in a restaurant, but not as a chef. She was the one doing the dishes. However, step-by-step, her talent was seen by the head chef when she was helping out with the basic cooking. By the request of the chef, she started to work as his assistant. So, her lessons started at that time. After 3 years of working in a restaurant as an assistant, she was finally able to go to the cooking academy.

After finishing the academy and with the help of her previous experience her career had a very good push. So, instead of working in restaurants she created recipes and menus for even the most famous bars, restaurants, and hotels in her city, Denver, CO.

But creating menus wasn't that much fulfilling. She wanted everyone in the world to try her recipes. So she started to create new recipes. The best way for everyone in the world to try the unique and easy meals she made. The best way to do that was through books. You can find many different recipes in her books, even traditional ones that most people have already forgotten about.

Getting even one of her books will draw you closer to your kitchen and maybe the recipes will be your inspiration to work on your culinary career.